GW00863425

A Student's Handbook

# LAMDA
# Speaking in
# Public

Acknowledgements

To my family

Thank you also to all my students who have worked
hard and provided the wonderful examples that I have
used in this book.

Additionally, I would like to thank Sarah Bostock,
Nicki Collins & Dave Fawbert for their support with
this book.

Cover Photo – Phillip Morgan

# Contents

# Who am I?

Hi, I'm Coral and I have been preparing students for LAMDA exams for over 12 years now following my time served as a Head of Drama in a large secondary school. I left traditional classroom teaching to pursue my dream to run my own drama school, Stages School of Acting, which has been running since 2012. As I had taken the LAMDA Acting exams myself as a teen I was keen to offer them to my students too, knowing how beneficial they are to developing skills and confidence. I have since taught in a preparatory school in Walsall, covering their LAMDA teacher's maternity leave. During which time I prepared almost 200 students for exams in Verse and Prose with 90% passing with Distinctions and 10% with Merits. In 2016, I was invited to offer LAMDA lessons at King Edward VI Five Ways Grammar school, as a perfect complement to their ever-growing extra-curricular opportunities. LAMDA lessons were a wonderful chance to develop greater confidence in the students' speaking skills.

I began to offer lessons in Speaking in Public, Acting, Verse & Prose, Devising, Reading for Performance and their most recent exam Shakespeare. The results have been remarkable 83% Distinctions and 17% Merits but my focus has always been primarily on developing the skills with students rather than simply preparing to jump through hoops in order to gain a certificate or medal. It is wonderful when students come to me excited about an awesome speech they have just delivered in English or a great performance in their drama class. This is why I love my job!

In 2020, the year that was primarily taken over by lockdown due to the Coronavirus Pandemic, I continued to tutor my LAMDA students online and even entered them for our first remote exams, again with amazing results. I also set up training events to help new teachers looking to offer LAMDA lessons to their students and a support group for them…Oh and I wrote this book!

The idea of this book is as a partner to the practical LAMDA Speaking in Public lessons in school from Grade 1-8. It will aid as a reminder of points covered in class and provide practical exercises to follow at home.

Thank you for purchasing this book and well done on making the decision to start your LAMDA journey!

# What is public speaking and why is it an important skill?

Public speaking is not, as many assume, always about addressing huge auditoriums packed to capacity as you may see in Ted Talks videos. Let's face it, how often are we likely to be in that sort of scenario? Sometimes public speaking can take the form of delivering a message in assembly, addressing your class in your English speaking and listening assessment, appealing to the board of school governors for a refurbishment of the toilet block. Public speaking may be in a college or university interview when they have required a presentation, or in front of a class to share ideas or even teach.

All of these scenarios seem far more likely to crop up in your lifetime and are excellent reasons for you to develop the confidence and skills to be the best you can be at it. How frustrating must it be to have a speech or presentation packed full of excellent points and inspirational insights but then lack the confidence to look up from your piece of paper to actually engage and deliver it to your audience?

Public speaking is not just an activity for the elite to indulge in at large corporate or social events, it is an essential skill that is used daily at all levels of interaction, from conversations and meetings to presentations and training events. Speaking to others effectively allows us to form connections, influence decisions and motivate change. Without the power of words and the ability to convey ideas coherently, the possibility of progress in the working world and life in general would be nearly impossible. Public speaking requires enthusiasm, communication skills, use of rhetoric and the ability to engage with an audience.

What are the benefits of developing my public speaking skills?

Effective Public speaking skills can help with career advancement, as they convey creativity, critical thinking, leadership abilities and professionalism; qualities that are valuable in the job market and life in general.

Public speaking is one of the most important and dreaded forms of communication.

# Why Public speaking is scary

## (and what you can do about it)

"According to most studies, people's number one fear is public speaking. Number two is death. Death is number two. Does that sound right? This means to the average person, if you go to a funeral, you're better off in the casket than doing the eulogy."

— Jerry Seinfeld

Fear is absolutely natural and you are not alone, the joke says it all... Generally, there is a fear around public speaking. Look at what could go wrong, I could forget what I am saying and then the audience will laugh at me? Maybe they'll come after me with pitchforks? You and I both know that isn't true so why do people dread public speaking so much? Why do our heartbeats race, our palms become sweaty and our throats become tight?

Our natural response goes right back to our fight or flight instincts; we are faced with our 'sabre toothed tiger' who has suddenly jumped out of the bushes and startled us.

Our body goes into overdrive. "Run, run away as fast as you can!" Throughout this book you will learn how to stand your ground and be equipped with the tools to keep that 'sabre-toothed tiger' at bay.

One of the most important things to do is IDENTIFY the problem. Here are the most common reasons people fear public speaking, see if you can relate to them.

## 1: Being Judged

People form opinions about everyone they come into contact with, you do it too! Before you even open your mouth to utter your first word you are being judged. This does not always mean in a negative way, they are judging whether they like you, so smile, make eye contact. They are judging whether you look like you know what you are talking about or out of your depth. So, walk confidently and with purpose. This is

YOUR space, YOUR time. YOU hold the key, the secret to enlightenment that your audience are in need of. Now doesn't that feel better already?

**Accept that you will be judged - so what?**

If they could do better, they would be standing up here instead. In fact, there was a story of a speaker who went out on stage and the first thing he did was make eye contact with various members of his audience, smiled at them and told them that "stuck under one of your seats is a piece of paper with a cross on it. The person with the cross will then come to the front and give a 2-minute speech on a topic of his or her choice. Exciting huh?" Well, of course the audience all stood and looked under their seats tentatively, each one desperately hoping it wasn't theirs. With a sigh of relief each sat back down.

He then told them that there was in fact no piece of paper with a cross on it at all, but asked how they felt when they thought they may have to deliver a speech in a minute. All would agree it was terrifying and had even started getting sweaty palms and tight throats at the prospect.

It IS daunting, anyone who tells you it isn't is either lying to you or as mad as the Hatter. The point is you are up doing something that your audience are terrified to do themselves.

## 2: Being found out – Imposter Syndrome

We ALL have it, we really do. Even if we are pretty much the experts in our field, we feel we don't know enough and we are winging it. You are not a fraud if you have done your homework and know your stuff; Which means knowing your subject above and beyond your isolated speech. How do you do this? From lots and lots of research.

Discussions, documentaries, books and specialist magazines as well as the wealth available on the internet means we can feel assured we have a good rounded knowledge of our subject matter.

## 3: Making a mistake and looking a fool

Not wanting to make a mistake in front of people is totally understandable. It could be mispronouncing a word, forgetting something or numerous other things you consider a mistake. The point is, unless you are a robot you are human, and humans make mistakes. Even Obama, a fantastic orator has made mistakes in his speeches and his audience love him all the more for it. The issue is not the mistake but how you react or recover from it; acknowledge it and keep going.

Is it easy to overcome these fears? Maybe not easy but certainly possible.

**Don't hide**

This means not hiding behind a lectern, your notes, a slide deck presentation or a false persona. Your audience are here to see you, to hear your thoughts and what you have to say. The first step to winning your audience over to your side it to make a physical connection with them and get them to like you.

Maya Angelou once said,

*"people will forget what you said, they will forget what you did but they will never forget how you made them feel."*

## Your mindset

Your mind is your most important asset – it is as if your body only exists to transport your brain around from place to place - What a clever organ it is!
Your frame of mind or mindset is the most important aspect to approaching your speech – if you start from a position of fear, fear of being judged or criticised you will hold back. Not only that but you will put yourself through the most gruelling trial too. Instead, you need to turn everything around 360.

Shift the power from your audience to you. They are not sitting there judging you from a position of authority but rather they have to come to learn something from you. To use a Star Wars analogy, imagine you are Yoda imparting wisdom to an audience of Luke Skywalkers; who will take their new-found knowledge and go and change the world. Now, you have become the guru, the authority figure... You have the power and the knowledge that your audience members are keen to learn. It's how you view the situation and your mindset that makes all the difference.

# WHAT ARE LAMDA EXAMS?

"Teachers from all over the world choose LAMDA Exams for their learners, drawn by the world-class reputation for integrity and excellence, the constant drive for ingenuity and innovation, as well as the tangible effects on their learners. From giving reticent learners the confidence to find their voice, and transforming inexperienced performers into speakers, LAMDA Exams has proven itself worthy of the trust that thousands of teachers have placed in us."

LAMDA

LAMDA (The London Academy of Music and Dramatic Art) is one of the oldest drama schools in England with a reputation all around the world for excellence.

LAMDA exams are about the achievement of skills developed in a number of subjects. There are several different disciplines which include:

- **Communication**
  Verse & Prose, Reading for Performance and Speaking in Public

- **Performance**
  Acting, Devising and Mime

- **Shakespeare**

- **Musical Theatre**

These can be taken solo, duo or in a group.

Whichever route you choose to take, you can feel assured that LAMDA training and exams have been empowering students to become confident speakers since the 1880s.

24

The aim of LAMDA training, whilst developing self-esteem and performance skills, is always to have fun doing so and I have written this book to help you achieve just that!

Understanding the Grades

There are no set ages for the graded exams, instead it depends on where you are when you start. For example, if someone asked how to get to London, your first question in being able to help them would be "where are you coming from?" only then can you plan your journey. Remember this is not a race to get to Grade 8 but a journey where you learn many skills along the way. If your sole objective is to collect certificates and medals then please put this book down right now and step away. If, however, you want to develop the skills to become a better, more confident and articulate public speaker, then read on!

## Grades

- Entry

- Level 1 – Grades 1-3

- Level 2 – Grades 4-5

- Level 3 – Grades 6-8

The time it takes to work towards each level depends on the work you decide to put in between lessons. There are suggested GLH (Guided learning hours) but it does depend on you practicing and preparing each week, keeping up with your vocal exercises and attending your lessons regularly.

Marking

Scores are broken into Interpretation and Technique; the marks vary depending on how much is required of you at that level but they are all out of 100.

The boundary marks are:

- Pass 50-64

- Merit 65-79

- Distinction 80+

## UCAS POINTS

Higher grades (6-8, Bronze, silver and Gold medal) also award UCAS points which can assist with applications to University.
To put the allocation of points into perspective, a Distinction at Grade 8 awards a whopping 30 points, which is equivalent to a C at A level. It really could make the difference of getting into one University or another.

It must be noted that not all universities accept UCAS points as part of their selection process. However, having extra skills and achievements are always noteworthy in an interview, and can set you apart from the other candidates. We all know that there is tough competition for places on courses so most universities are looking beyond your academic achievements and more towards your extracurricular skills. LAMDA is widely acknowledged as a reputable qualification to achieve.

It is important to understand that UCAS points cannot be accumulated within the same discipline. For example, Verse & Prose, Reading for Performance and Speaking in Public are all under the discipline "Communication" so only the highest grade's points will be awarded.

However, if you also had achieved in another discipline such as "Performance" those points would be added together.

These tables show the amount of UCAS points awarded for a Pass, Merit or Distinction at each of the Level 3 graded exams.

| COMMUNICATION | Grade 6 | Grade 7 | Grade 8 |
|---|---|---|---|
| Pass | 8 | 12 | 24 |
| Merit | 10 | 14 | 27 |
| Distinction | 12 | 16 | 30 |

| PERFORMANCE | Grade 6 | Grade 7 | Grade 8 |
|---|---|---|---|
| Pass | 8 | 12 | 24 |
| Merit | 10 | 14 | 27 |
| Distinction | 12 | 16 | 30 |

| MUSICAL THEATRE | Grade 6 | Grade 7 | Grade 8 |
|---|---|---|---|
| Pass | 8 | 12 | 24 |
| Merit | 10 | 14 | 27 |
| Distinction | 12 | 16 | 30 |

| SHAKESPEARE | Level 3 |
|---|---|
| Pass | 4 |
| Merit | 8 |
| Distinction | 12 |

# Speaking with Gravitas

**So, what exactly is Gravitas?**

Gravitas is translated as weight, seriousness, solemnity, dignity, and importance.

People who speak with gravitas seem to have the world eating out of the palm of their hands; they command respect from those who listen to them, because they have taken the time to really *think* and *plan* what they are going to say. Their thoughts are calm, logical and delivered in a measured manner. People who communicate with gravitas emotionally moves their audiences and inspires them to take action.

Is it the tone of your voice? Is it the way you carry yourself? The way you stand? The connection you make with your audience? Or is it something you acquire with practice?

The answer is – all of the above.
Some people are born with a natural ability to communicate with flair and personality, but this does not mean that it cannot be learned by all.

There are certain qualities you need to focus on to develop gravitas.

- Self-awareness
- Expertise
- Authenticity
- Presence
- Connection
- Projection

Out of these, the most important when it comes to public speaking are presence, connection, and projection. These are the fundamental attributes in gaining an audience's attention and trust. Presence can be summed up as an energy that emanates from a person through physical appearance, body language, and voice. Connection is an affinity with people and the art of creating rapport with any audience. Projection is the ability to 'switch on' your best self, not only projecting your voice but mental projection of your personality. If you want your speech to be taken seriously, give it the time it deserves. Plan, prepare, structure, build in pauses, breathe deeply into your Diaphragm and use breath force to give your speech strength (not necessarily volume).

Diaphragmatic breathing and breath control have the effect of lowering the depth of your voice and bringing more resonance to your delivery, which people will find reassuring, particularly if your message is a challenging one. More information on breathing, resonance & breath control will be explored later.

# Creating a speech:

# Intention and Audience

What to create a speech about?

If you have not been given a topic but rather to find your own, do what Ted Talks do and find an 'Idea that matters'. What is it that matters to you? What do you feel passionately about? What are you interested in? If you have a blasé attitude towards your subject why would anyone else care? Surely, we want them to care or else what would be the point of them giving you 4 minutes of their life? When you think of it like that, they are giving their time... Teach them something, make them. Look at something from another angle, enlighten them.

I make no secret of the fact that there are often times when a student would come to me with an idea that they feel passionate about, that I wouldn't have a clue about! For example, I have had students with extensive knowledge of the universe, aviation or trains, none of which I am well versed in but you can bet your bottom dollar I knew a lot more after these speeches. I am sure I learn as much from my students as they do from me.

So, find that subject that makes you buzz or maybe enrages you... Listen to your heart. When you speak from your heart rather than your head is when the magic happens!

Find your intention and your audience

Your purpose or intention is very important in a speech, it is the sole reason for delivering a speech; to have some sort of impact. Look at it as your destination, without a fixed point of focus your journey could take all sorts of twists and turns, rambling on. I'm sure you've sat through a few of those sorts of speeches.

Let's imagine you are about to take a journey, your speech. If you know you are taking a train journey (your topic) but you have no idea where you are going, your destination is unknown, and you could end up anywhere. So, what IS the purpose of your speech? Is it to inform or educate your audience on a specific topic? I recently had a student work on an informative speech based on Star Wars, the history of it, characters, plot, music and technical wizardry. Another student told me all about Trading Card Games (TCG) and how they

39

have evolved to worldwide championships being played with huge cash prizes! You can even assume a role to deliver your speech in the latter example, this student assumed the role of a TCG champion.

To help you decide on a suitable approach, decide whether your speech is to be educational, informative, or persuasive. Refer to the following 4 rhetorical devices;

**Logos** – an appeal to logic
**Pathos** – an appeal to emotion
**Ethos** – an appeal to ethics
**Kairos** – an appeal to time

Rhetorical devices are used throughout literature, the types of words you choose have a different effect on the reader or in this case listener. For example, "The monster lurched towards the boy" creates a far more dramatic or emotional response in the audience than "The monster walked towards the boy". I am sure you have started to look at this in your English lessons already, so you get the picture. I will talk more about rhetorical strategies. in Verbal Communication later. Needless to say, you need to pinpoint your intention, your purpose and then your target audience. If you don't know to whom you are addressing how will you know what to include and how to present your topic?

The students who created the speeches on Star Wars or Trading Card Games had a very clear purpose and audience. The first was delivered to a film society, to give some context to the film before it was shown. The second speech on Trading Card Games was to appeal to other teens to encourage them to put down the electronics and take up the activity, more specifically to join his society.

To script or not to script?

There are many schools of thought on this one. I would always suggest that you never script your entire speech word for word. Why? Yes, it would give you a safety net but think about it, you are on stage, delivering a speech. You need to engage with your audience, make eye contact but your eyes are always drawn down to your script. You do however momentarily glance up to smile and connect but when you look down at the sea of text you have trouble finding where you are!
Not only that but most importantly your speech sounds rehearsed, robotic and characterless. Take a listen to speeches on Ted Talks and Toastmasters and hear how fluent and spontaneous they sound. You need to appear as though you are giving that speech for the first time not the hundredth.

It is more important to know what you are talking about than what you are saying.

What do I mean by this? Simply, know your subject, and do your research so that you can talk confidently about it not be tied to a script.

What if I forget what I am saying?
This is why you have markers along the way, strategic points that prompt your next idea; these are what you would pop down on note cards.

Think of it as acting. Play with it a little bit. Try to keep it loose. It's imperative that you don't lose the natural aspect of the speech.

Non-verbal Communication

An audience decides within seconds if they trust the speaker on stage. These seconds are used to take in a lot of information before he or she even utters their first word. How does the speaker present themselves? Are they connecting with me through eye contact? Do they look as though they are happy to be there and actually want to talk to me?

If The audience don't trust the speaker immediately, it won't matter what they say, they will not be persuaded.

Body language is part of non-verbal communication. It is the combination of movements, gestures, and postures; this includes the way a speaker talks, moves and looks on stage. Body language is part of the message a speaker wants to give. Why is body language important? You can say that having the wrong body language can prevent your speech from being a success. You need a lot of talent in other elements of your speech to make up for bad or misleading body language.

Some examples of bad body language include:

- Turning your back to the audience
- Moving around too much or hiding behind a desk or lectern.
- Unsuitable gesturing can also have a negative influence on your talk.
- Being too aggressive in your gestures, drumming your fingers or even biting your nails.

Even when you are doing a good job, making small improvements in your body language can have a big effect on the way the audience receives your talk. It can make the difference between a nice talk which is enjoyed and then instantly forgotten and actually persuading people to change their way of thinking. This is why it is so important for everyone to pay attention to how much energy are you putting into your talk. Too little energy will make your audience fall asleep. Then again, too much will make them less interested in your message!

Stance

How you stand says a lot about your confidence in yourself, your message and therefore how much confidence your audience should have in you.

Aim to place feet hip width apart and keep back up straight, shoulders back and head balanced on top, neither bending forward or leaning back – either of which will constrict your voice. You need to make sure that there is no tension in the body that will not only restrict your voice but make movements stiff and robotic. Make sure you do your stretches first.

Gait

To walk or not to walk, that is the question!
It is always better for your audience when
use the space available appropriately; what
a waste to stand rigid in one spot or hidden
behind a lectern. You may find some
moments of walking are helpful to the flow
and rhythm of your speech but it has to
come from instinct and not be rigidly set to
lines. Think about moving to a new space
for each new idea or what would be a new
paragraph in an English essay. This is also
a good way of ensuring you are connecting
and engaging with your audience; being
physically closer at times can encourage
making them feel emotionally involved.
Why not practice simply walking onto
stage confidently and saying "Good
Afternoon, my name is...." and just keep
practicing until it feels comfortable.

Good body language can be trained. You
can do this by rehearsing or practicing in

front of colleagues, or better still, video yourself and watch back. Do you look and sound how you think you should?

Use open body language as much as possible. What does that mean? Try not to have any physical barriers between you and your audience. This could be a lectern; if possible, step out and away from it and the space available.

Eye contact

It is not only important to connect with your audience, but it is essential for them to feel you are speaking directly to them. Imagine a speaker, with the most interesting speech in the world delivering it to the ground or to his or her notecards, you would soon disengage.

Of course, there is making eye contact and then there is entering into a staring competition and intimidating your audience member. So; the secret is to catch their eye and engage briefly with one person before moving to the next. If you have a large audience use the "windscreen wiper effect" stopping for 2-3 seconds on different areas left, right, centre at front and the same at back. Try not to make it mechanical and predictable… this will also keep your audience members on their toes, you could be looking at them next!

Use of notecards

Notecards are a good support, a means of reminding you what comes next, but they are merely that, reminders or prompts, NOT the speech. If the speech is written on the cards or any prompts too lengthy, you will spend more time looking at or reading off your cards than connecting with your audience. Remember the 90/10 rule – you should spend 90% of your time looking at and connecting with the audience and only 10% looking at your cards or Visual Aids.

If your speech is written fully line by line, you risk sounding like a robot. It is about knowing what you are talking about rather than exactly what you are saying, word for word. This way there is the flexibility for you to be fluid with your expression, not become an automaton; people like real people!

Gestures

What gestures are you making? Are you using your hands and not hiding them in your pockets? Are you pointing? being expressive?

If someone has ever made fun of you for making elaborate hand gestures while talking; or if you've seen footage of yourself speaking only to be horrified by your flailing forearms, don't be too concerned. According to psychologists, those gestures are probably helping you express your thoughts more effectively.

Hand gestures are a really powerful aspect of communication, for both the speaker and the listener. A study analysing TED Talks last year found that the most popular viral speakers used an average of about 465 hand gestures, which is nearly twice as many as the least popular speakers used. Other research has found that people who "talk" with their hands tend to be viewed as warm, agreeable and energetic, while those who are less animated are seen as logical, cold and analytical.

Having open palms, faced upwards is the best way for an audience to trust you and have faith and confidence in what you are saying. You may notice there are a few politicians who always deliver speeches with closed fists… I will leave that one with you. The palms are a soft weak spot and when you show them, it psychologically indicates that you are open and honest, worthy of our trust. Your audience are then likely to feel you are genuine, truthful and well-meaning.

Research shows that audiences tend to view people who use a greater variety of gestures in a more favourable light. Studies have found that people who communicate through active gesturing tend to be evaluated as warm, agreeable and energetic, while those who remain still (or whose gestures seem mechanical or "wooden") are seen as logical, cold, and analytical.

That's one of the reasons why gestures are so critical to a leader and why getting them right in a presentation connects powerfully with an audience.

Congruence

Trust is established through congruence; that perfect alignment between what is being said, and the body language that accompanies it. If a speaker's gestures are not in full agreement with the spoken words, the audience consciously or subconsciously perceives duplicity, uncertainty or (at the very least) internal conflict.

## I say umm or err a lot, how can I control this?

Audiences love speakers who are in control. If a speaker shows strength, the audience are quicker to believe the speaker. This means standing up straight and powerful, but also learning how to avoid saying stop-words like "uhm" all the time.

How often do you say "um" or "Err" when you talk? Probably a lot; because many people do. These words are called "filler words". But what effect do these filler words have on your speech and how can you fix this?

When you use filler words, your speech stops being fluent and flowing freely but instead can become quite staccato. Your audience will assume that you are not too confident about what you are saying. When you Umm or Errr you are verbalising that you need a moment to think "where am I?" but you don't want that awkward silence. Well you know what? That silence is not awkward, it's great (see Pauses). Instead try saying nothing, just pause. This is a great opportunity for your audience to process what you have just said and for you to take a breath, glance (and I mean glance) at notecards or to move into new space.

It will sound less weird than you think and although at first you may feel it is a long silence it is a pause the audience will appreciate.

So, don't 'Umm', use a pause instead, I love... pauses.

# Presentation

**"It ain't what you say it's the way that you say it"**

Bananarama

Your audience start taking in information from the moment you step into view. They decide whether they like you or not and whether if you are worth listening to before you've even uttered your first word. Harsh but true, so it demonstrates just how important presentation is. You could have the most informative speech content wise, but if you deliver it in a monotone or monotonous voice, or hidden behind a lectern or reading from your notes, your audience won't stay awake long enough to hear it; it will not hit home and you are wasting both your own and your audience's time.

Variation / modulation

Firstly, let's look at how we can keep our voices engaging.

The brain is wired to tap into 'change'. If a speech is on one level, or at one tone or pace or volume, it can, for the listener, soon become tiring and they will disengage.

We need to mix things up a little, after all 'variety is the spice of life' as they say. We can 'shift gears' in a speech by changing any of our 4Ps when approaching a new idea.

The 4 Ps - Pitch, Pace, Pause, Power

Pitch:
The highness or lowness of the note on which you speak. A piece of music on one note would soon become dull and boring... you get the hint. Vary your pitch at least with each new idea; high – conveys a light & happy tone whereas low is more of a sombre or solemn one. It's not rocket science, yet many people overlook this really important technique. Use pitch to support the mood you wish to convey.

To avoid sounding monotonous try to envisage a landing with stairs going down to the ground floor and another set of stairs going up to the loft. Don't just stay on the landing but imagine with each new idea you are going somewhere, either up or down. You can stay on the landing for a while but not too long.

**Inflection:**
Inflection is the rise and fall of your voice, it reflects your personality. It should not require conscious thought or your speech will become stilted. Take care towards the end of sentences not to throw away the last few words. The last word should be as supported as your first. Falling inflection works for statements and commands and a rising inflection, interest, surprise or questions. Try it.

**Tonal register / tone:** The light and shade of your voice. Projecting emotion. Mark it on your speech what emotion you want to convey and where.

Does your speech require a light, bouncy, fun tone because we are talking about something positive, or does it require a more mysterious or sombre tone? The tone needs to match your content or you may find your audience becoming confused.

Pace:
Pace is the speed you speak at, try and vary it to convey meaning and mood.

Nothing indicates nervousness more than racing through your presentation. If you want to impact the audience in a meaningful way, make sure they actually hear what you are saying. Slow it down but make sure that they can actually keep up. Vary your pace with each new idea.

**Slower:** Lengthening words and the gaps between. Words suggesting size, effort, astonishment and long periods of time can be lengthened. Exotic words for the audience to ponder or emotional phrases can be taken at a slower pace. A phrase that contains many short ideas can be slowed down as can a series of short sentences.

**Faster**: Shorter words and fewer gaps lead to a faster pace; which can be great to convey excitement. Additionally, an increase of pace can build to a climax. Use this technique when not saying anything complex that the audience needs to process, reflect on or consider. Most new students tend to speak too quickly rather than too slowly because nerves make us rattle through things like a runaway train rather than pace ourselves. Be conscious of this drive and aim to control your pace.

Pause:
When sound... Stops!

A very underrated feature and my particular favourite. The pause can be so powerful, it may be the absence of words but it is certainly not the absence of meaning.

Pausing is very useful for several reasons;

**Thinking time for them**: It is difficult to follow a speaker who talks continuously, so it is a moment for the audience to process what you have just said; especially if you have given some complex information or asked a rhetorical question. Give them time to think

**Thinking time for you**:  This is a moment for you to change energy and tone; and gives you a little break before introducing your next idea. A perfect time to glance at your note cards.

**A chance to breathe:** You know you need a good lungful of air to project your next sentence and give it some energy. So, take

the pause as a moment to 'fill up' then push
out next sentence with oomph!

**To emphasise**: A momentary silence is
very strong and draws the audience's
attention to what you have said or keep
them in suspense over what you are about
to say; like a rollercoaster hovering before
the big dip, so pause before or after a word
or phrase to make it stand out. It is
therefore isolated. Be careful, holding a
pause too long can break the spell.

**Emotional pause**: The voice is suspended
by emotion; this needs to be used subtly or
can appear over dramatic.

Power:
This is the stress, the breath force that you
put behind a word. It is the verbal
equivalent to underlining the word, to draw
attention and 'value' to its prominence.
There are 'penny' words and there are
'pound' words, if that makes sense? The

63

penny words are important to hold the sentence together and must still be delivered clearly. The pound words are the key words that show us what is important. We can draw attention to these by focussing on the 4P's.

Try saying the following out loud a few times and each time changing your pitch higher or lower on the word SAT.

The cat **sat** on the mat

It didn't lie or stand but it **sat.**

Now try it again, but this time using greater stress / force on SAT. Then, try it again by adding a pause before/after the word SAT. Then elongate or lengthen the word SAT.

Whichever way you try it, you have certainly made a point about what the cat was doing on the mat!

# Exercises

Stretches:

1. Reach your arms up to the ceiling as high as you can... no, even higher than that - really stretch on tip toes and right to the ends of each finger.

2. Leaving your fingers where they are, slowly lower your heels - this will stretch your spine.

3. Slightly bend the knees, nice and soft, so you don't lock them back and let your upper body flop over from the waist, just like a puppet whose strings have been cut. Just hang there for a few seconds, feel the release of weight as you just hang or swing slowly side to side.

4. Gradually, uncurl your spine, vertebra by vertebra as you slowly return to standing.

5. Stretch your arms out to the sides, try and reach both walls, stretch right to the ends of your fingers again and then lean over to the right side, arm above your head, stretching your ribcage and the intercostal muscles.

6. Repeat this on the other side so that the ribcage can move up and outwards easily.

Your voice

It is very important to look after your voice and to do this, you need to remain hydrated, drink plenty of water. You must also avoid screaming or shouting and straining your larynx.

Warm up properly - As you can imagine an athlete cannot go out onto the track and break into a sprint, they would damage their muscles. They need to warm up the muscles they are about to use. Similarly, with speaking you need to do the same and warm up your muscles and release any tension in your body face and throat that may constrict your voice. You must aim to support your voice with breath support when you speak rather than straining the larynx.

Breathing

Yes, yes, I know we have been breathing since the day we were born, it is an involuntary action. However, when it comes to speaking, singing, playing an instrument and many other activities; you need to develop breath control and it needs to be a more conscious thing.

Most people aren't really conscious of the way they're breathing, but generally, there are three types of breathing patterns:

- Thoracic (chest) breathing
- Clavicular (shoulders)
- Diaphragmatic (abdominal) breathing

When people are anxious, they tend to take rapid, shallow breaths that come directly from the chest. This type of breathing is called thoracic or chest breathing. When you're feeling anxious, you may not even be aware you're breathing this way. However, chest breathing causes an upset in the oxygen and carbon dioxide levels in the body resulting in an increased heart rate. When someone is very distraught and tearful, they use clavicular breathing, which is even shorter, sharper shallow breaths but during diaphragmatic breathing you take deep, even breaths; this is the way new-born babies naturally breathe. You're also probably using this pattern of breathing when you're in a relaxed stage of sleep.

**Thoracic breathing vs. Abdominal breathing**

The easiest way to determine your breathing pattern is to put one hand on your upper abdomen near the waist and the other in the middle of your chest. As you breathe, notice which hand raises the most.

If you're breathing properly, your abdomen should expand and contract with each breath (and the hand on it should raise the most). It's especially important to be aware of these differences during stressful and anxious times when you're more likely to breathe from your chest.

Simple Breathing Exercises

The next time you're feeling anxious try this simple relaxation technique:

- **Inhale slowly and deeply** Keep your shoulders relaxed. Your abdomen should expand and your chest should rise very little.
- **Exhale slowly** As you blow air out, purse your lips slightly but keep your jaw relaxed. You may hear a soft "whooshing" sound as you exhale.
- **Repeat this breathing exercise**. Do it for several minutes

Projection

Projection means to "send out". The projector in your classroom sends or throws out an image onto a board. Similarly, when delivering a speech, you need to send out your voice right to the back of the hall.

Let's imagine Granny, who has hearing difficulties, is sat at the back of the hall. She needs your voice to travel all the way to her. How do you do this without 'shouting'? Firstly, that will damage your vocal cords and secondly it sounds awful! So, we need to be louder, we need to 'speak from our diaphragm' but what does that really mean?

Where is your Diaphragm?

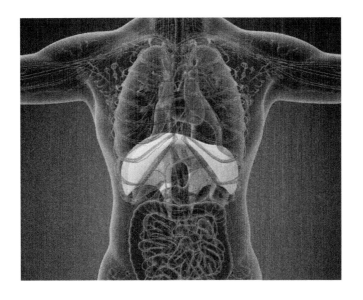

Your Diaphragm is a band of muscle located beneath your ribcage. It is constantly contracting and relaxing in order for you to breathe. However, our normal daily breathing is quite different from the type of breathing we need to use when we are addressing an audience. We need our voice to project further and this will mean engaging three sets of muscles; the

Intercostal Muscles, the Diaphragm and the Abdominal muscles.

I always compare speaking from your diaphragm or diaphragmatic breathing to your garden hose. Imagine if you just turn your tap on slightly, there would be water coming out of the hose, but it would trickle out and not travel very far. What do we need to do to get the water to reach further? You turn the tap more so there is greater pressure behind the water. More water and greater pressure will ensure that the roses at the bottom of the garden are watered. So, now imagine the water is air and the hose is your Trachea or Windpipe, the tap is therefore your Diaphragm and Abdominal muscles. The more air you take in and the more force applied by the diaphragm and abs to send it back out, the further it will travel. So, learning good breathing techniques and control is key to being a good speaker and ensuring Granny at the back can hear you.

**What is breath control?**

Breath control, as the name suggests, is controlling the amount of breath you take and the force behind it as it is released. This affects the strength behind your voice when you are speaking. Releasing too much air too quickly will result in you running out of air before the end of your sentence; this makes the voice fade or sound weaker and leads to a falling inflection. You want all your words to have the same strength behind them right until the full stop.

Breathing exercises to develop **breath control**

- Breath in for 4 hold for 4 then release on a "shhhh" sound for 8

- Breath in for 2 hold for 4 then release on a "shhhh" sound for 10
- Breath in for 1 hold for 4 then release on a "shhhh" sound for 12

Perfect!

Hopefully, you now understand the importance of breath control and how it assists projection; and you also have some exercises to improve this. There are many more you can find online. I strongly recommend following the National Theatre vocal exercises that can be found on YouTube.

Articulation

Granny at the back can now hear you, you are audible but are you intelligible? Can she understand what you are saying? Are your words crisp and clear? If not, that is where articulation comes in, often referred to as clarity.

To articulate or to have clarity of speech you need to make sure that you open your mouth to let the sound come out, try speaking now with your mouth closed, the sound stays trapped there right? Open the door, open it wide. To help you do this we need to reduce any tension in the face, jaw and tongue. Here are some exercises to warm up those muscles.

Take your two fingers on each hand and massage the muscles around the mandible / jaw line. Just little circles moving along the jaw ready for our lion and lemon faces!

"Lion face / lemon face" – 'Lion' face is opening your eyes and mouth as wide as you can as if a lion has jumped out in front of you. 'Lemon' face imagine you have sucked on a bitter lemon and your face squeezes as small as possible. 'Lion face, lemon face' – repeat stretching the muscles one way and then the other.

Sticky toffee – pop an imaginary sticky toffee into your mouth and start to chew and chew, moving it around your mouth. It is very sticky and often gets stuck in your teeth so try and get it out using your tongue.

Tongue exercises – stick your tongue out as far as you can, now move it all the way up, down, left, right (now clean all the dribble off your chin) and pop your tongue back!

Brush your teeth with your tongue, move it around the outside of your teeth in a clockwise motion and then anti-clockwise.

Now take a big deep breath and concentrate on the shape of your mouth, exaggerate even as you say slowly and clearly the 5 vowels.

# AEIOU

Now increase the speed to a normal speaking pace so that you say it twice but at double the speed.

## AEIOU AEIOU

Now three times as quickly and clearly as you can.

## AEIOU AEIOU AEIOU

Next, after the long open vowels we have, yes you guessed it, the consonants. These are the building blocks of words, the hard edges. If the vowels are a free running stream the consonants are the banks and rocks that shape the water's path. These are formed by different positions of the articulators, which are the lips, the teeth, the teeth ridge, the hard and soft palates.

So, let's try the "Consonant March."

Starting with the Plosives (These abrupt consonant sounds are produced by stopping the air by the lips, teeth or palate followed by a sudden release of air) These are P, B, T, D.

P, P, PPPP, PPP PPP PPPP
B,B, BBBB, BBB BBB BBBB
T, T, TTTT, TTT TTT TTTT
D,D, DDDD, DDD DDD DDDD

Great, now you can choose some more consonants. Start slowly to make sure you are forming the letter sounds correctly and saying them clearly. Then you can gradually speed up. Remember, Accuracy before speed!

This is also the case with **Tongue Twisters**; Here is a good selection for you to dip into and mix them up to keep your warm up fun

*Red Lorry, Yellow Lorry*
*Red Leather, Yellow Leather*

*Unique New York, Unique New York we all adore Unique New York*

*Seventy-Seven Benevolent Elephants*

*If a dog chews shoes, whose shoes does he choose?*

*Always choose stew on Tuesdays, because Tuesdays are stew days.*

*Black Background, Brown Background*

*A Big black bug bit a big black bear*

*Peter Piper Picked a Peck of Pickled Peppers, If Peter Piper picked a peck of pickled peppers, where's the peck of pickled peppers Peter Piper picked?*

*A box of biscuits, a box of mixed biscuits and a biscuit mixer*

*I saw a kitten eating chicken in the kitchen*

*Flash message (x3)*

*Black background, brown background (x3)*

*There's no need to light a night light on a light night like tonight*

*To begin to toboggan, first buy a toboggan but don't buy too big a toboggan because too big a toboggan is too big a toboggan to buy to begin to toboggan!*

*Amidst the mists and coldest frosts With stoutest wrists and firmest boasts*

*He thrusts his fists against the posts*
*And still insists he sees the ghosts*

*Articulation is a form of gymnastics*
*between the lips, the teeth and the tip of the*
*tongue, the tip of the tongue, the teeth and*
*the lips; for example:*

*I want a proper cup of coffee from a proper*
*copper coffee pot*

# PREPARING YOUR SPEECH

## Topic

Your topic not only has to be of interest to your audience but most importantly to you. If you have no opinion on it there will be no passion and a speech without passion is, well…you've heard them before. Your eyes glaze over and your mind easily wanders. However, the talk that is fuelled by energy, that twists and turns and has you thinking throughout, is the speech that has you on the edge of your seat.

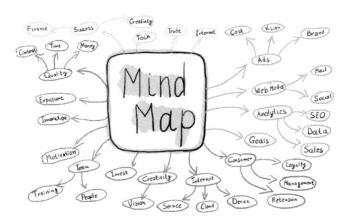

**Mind Map**: The first thing to do is to grab a piece of paper and write down everything you already know about the topic, different ideas you want to explore. Now you have emptied your mind, look at the mind map. Do any areas look like they could combine or support each other? Indicate these with a marker. Do any areas pop out at you as the area of that topic you would like to pursue further in your speech? They do? Great move onto step 2 – if not then perhaps this topic isn't suitable...think of another and try the mind map again.

**Research:** Learn more about your chosen area. This doesn't only mean searching the internet, although the internet is a great resource but also watch documentaries, read books and specialist magazines, talk to people who know about this topic. Learn, learn, learn and be like a squirrel collecting nuts.

Now you have a wealth of info on your chosen subject area. Hopefully, you have collected many quotes, statistics and examples to help back up your viewpoint. So, what to do now, there's far too much?

**Categorise**: Place all your information on post-it notes and group together in similar categories. You will find that some areas go well together and support each other or lead naturally onto another area.

**Purpose**: Decide on the purpose of your speech, what do you want to convey? You only have a few minutes so it's unlikely you can mention everything on the topic. Be specific, be purposeful. Refer back to 'intention' in that we covered earlier in the book.

For example: My topic may be endangered species but how I choose to deliver that, what to include will depend on my purpose. Do I want to draw attention to one particular species? or do I want my audience to donate to a charity? Or do I want them to stop buying certain products? Once I have decided on my purpose, I need to think about who would this subject be most suitable for? 5-year olds? Probably not. For example, if my intention was to ask the audience to stop purchasing certain products because of the impact they have, such as products that contain Palm oil, I would need to look at who are the prime consumers of this? Who can make a difference? That's who I need to target. Which leads me seamlessly onto….

Audience

Know them! Ok….so you won't know them all personally by name, but you can do your homework. You could find yourself talking to people of all ages, from all walks of life and backgrounds as varied as their cultures. To target your audience as a generic, one size fits all audience is actually going to make creating your speech so much harder as different people need different information.

What demographic are they? Where from? What are likely to be their beliefs and opinions? What is their level of understanding or prior knowledge of this subject? i.e. an audience of 6-year olds will need to be addressed very differently to a medical panel so the most important thing after your purpose is pinpointing who needs to hear your message.

Alternatively, you could be asked to present a speech based on your audience…what do they need or want to know? What topics will be suitable for them and how will you pitch it correctly? A younger audience has a narrower concentration span so the pace needs to be energetic, bouncy but not too fast.

However, they do not want you to labour a point and aren't as interested in statistics or data. Your carefully presented graphs may go unappreciated with this particular audience. My initial topic might be animals, I then decide to target a younger audience of say 5 to 6-year olds. The appropriate approach at this age would be to focus on wild animals, dinosaurs or pets. Perhaps, "how to look after a pet". This may include walking, care, feeding etc. However, for an older audience I may take that topic of animals into focusing on extinction and how we can slow this down. A more mature audience is far more likely to benefit from statistics and data, therefore a slower more detailed approach would be required. However, the same topic of animals could still be the starting point, only this time it may be more appropriate to explore the extinction of certain species.

## Rhetorical devices - Language and terminology

Another reason why knowing your audience is so important before creating your speech, is that it helps determine the type of language and terminology you should use. Look at not only the level of understanding; but perhaps background or prior knowledge of this subject your audience may have. Are they completely new to this concept? In which case you have to start from scratch and explain thoroughly. However, if your topic is developing a concept the audience may already be familiar with, start from there. Additionally, if they are already aware of certain subject specific terminology and jargon then go ahead and use them.

Ok, so I have decided that my topic is of 'Animals' and my focus will be the impending extinction of the xxx

My audience are XXX and my purpose will be to encourage them to take action to help support the charities. _

Now, what rhetorical devices or strategies will help me convey this message most effectively? Am I appealing to logic, emotion, ethics or time?

Some strategies you could employ are:

- Alliteration
- Amplification
- Anadiplosis
- Antanagoge
- Chiasmus
- Euphemism
- Hypophora
- Similes

## Alliteration

Alliteration uses repetition in the initial consonant sound of a word or word phrase.

The consonant sound is repeated for most or all the words being used to convey a sense of lyricism, for example:

Freshly Fallen Flowers

In the example, the F consonant is repeated to turn a listener's attention to the event.

## Amplification

Amplification builds on a word, phrase or sentence, evoking a sense of urgency and intensity in the listener. For example:

They want a perfect house in a perfect neighbourhood.

The repetitive use of 'perfect' in the example highlights the importance of finding the right home and place to live.

## Anadiplosis

This device uses the same word at the end of a sentence and the beginning of the next sentence. Used this way, the anadiplosis allows a chain of thought to carry through to the next idea, allowing your audience to follow along with the point you are presenting. Using a repetitive approach allows the listener to follow along the path of your ideas. Here is a famous example of anadiplosis as the character Yoda uses it in Star Wars: The Empire Strikes Back: Fear leads to anger. Anger leads to fear. Fear leads to suffering.

Using this strategy can help to put more emphasis on the ideas being conveyed, stressing the importance of your points.

**Antanagoge**

An antanagoge uses both a negative and positive statement in one sentence or phrase. You can use this rhetorical device to present a problem and a subsequent solution. Consider the following, well-known example of antanagoge:

When life gives you lemons, make lemonade.

This quote conveys the negativity in having a bunch of lemons with its subsequent solution, making lemonade from all of it. Another example of common usage of the antanagoge device:

The house is old and worn, but it's clean and sturdy.

The device works here by presenting what could be considered a problem, and then providing a positive viewpoint (or solution) to the earlier negative statement. This can sometimes be a useful device in speeches.

## Chiasmus

Chiasmus is a rhetorical technique where the speaker changes the order of the words or phrases in a sentence to invoke a sense of powerful emotion. This device works by allowing the listener to have an emotional thought response to what is being said. One of the most well-known and powerful examples of this rhetorical device can be heard in President John F. Kennedy's inaugural speech:

"Ask not what your country can do for you; but what you can do for your country".

He used this device to provoke deep thought, as well as to make a personal connection between the population and their roles within the American nation.


**Euphemism**

Euphemism is a rhetorical device that uses a pleasant phrase or saying to convey a more familiar or less pleasant one. For example:

"Slum" could be described as "Culturally deprived environment"

"Cookery Lessons" could also be described as "Domestic science".

## Hypophora

This rhetorical strategy is used when a speaker asks a question and then immediately provides the answer. For example:

Why is it important to take breaks whilst revising? It is important because your hippocampus is in a better position to retain information.

Unlike a rhetorical question, a hypophora wastes no time in providing a direct answer to a posed question. With a rhetorical question I always suggest you pause briefly for the rhetorical answer occurring in the audience's minds.

## Similes

The simplest of the devices works by invoking a sense of comparison between two like subjects. Similes work to provide a comparable point-of-view to a well-known or familiar subject. For example:

He was as big as a house.

She was as quick as a fox.

The children were as loud as a herd of elephants

# Structuring your speech

You have decided on what your audience
wants or needs to know and now you need
to decide what is to be included.

**Filter**

Now you have a clear idea of the purpose
of your speech and audience it is targeted at
you can now start to filter the content.
Remove any ideas, no matter how
interesting, if they do not fit your purpose
and audience. What you have left is ideally
the key ingredients you should include in
your speech.

**Order**

Prioritise your key points from most
interesting and impactful down to the least
relevant. A good idea is to write each piece
of information on post-it notes and then
you can play around with the order of them.
Put those at the top which you will
definitely want to include, but remember,

the order in which you place them will be very important to ensure a fluent speech not one that jumps from one idea to another unrelated idea.

To structure your speech, just like a story you need a clear beginning, middle and end.

Draw three rectangular boxes on an A4 sheet of paper. At the top a smaller one for the 'hook' or introduction, a larger one for the body of the speech and another one a similar size to the first for the 'call to action' or 'conclusion'.

## HOOK

This is the introduction to your speech but how dull simply to say, "Good afternoon, my name is Colin Smith and I am going to talk about such and such". I think your audience may already be dropping off. Instead, think of this as your opportunity to connect with your audience, to make eye contact and smile (if appropriate, which it almost always is) and then to grab their attention and hook them in! Why not take some time to look at speeches on YouTube, Ted Talks and Toastmasters? Look at what devices the speakers use to 'hook' in their audiences' attentions. What examples do you like? Make a list of them as a bank to refer to when you are working on your hook. Is it the use of a prop? Quote? Rhetorical question, demonstration or action? Picture? Shocking statistic? Something that arouses your curiosity? Or an interactive situation?

One student of mine came on stage with an object that was covered... he did not refer to it immediately but kept our attention during the 'hook' as we all wanted to know what was under the cloth. Another student of mine always likes to begin his speeches with a roleplay, it's kind of his trademark now. A particular favourite of mine was a speech he gave looking at the ugly truth of online retail. The student entered the room with a box, stating excitedly that it was the item he had only just ordered this morning which had arrived already! He, went on to talk about what is involved for this to have possibly happened so quickly after pressing 'Buy now'. He explored the level of stress that selecting 'Buy now' causes to human beings, the warehouse staff and the delivery drivers. This leads us to consider whether we really needed that item right now or whether we could wait a few days and make everyone's life a little easier. The most impactful line was, "when you hit 'same day delivery' you set off a chain of human suffering."

So, the message here is to really think about how you want your audience to end up feeling, and how are you going to achieve this throughout the speech, starting with your hook?

## BODY

The body is a calmer affair. You have your audience in the palm of your hand with your gripping 'hook' and now you can take the time to explain or inform on your key points; this is where you will now show your research and your subject knowledge more fully.

## CALL TO ACTION

DO NOT start writing your speech at the very beginning. Instead, start with your ending, your 'call to action' – as this should be the most impactful part that the audience will take away with them. Get it wrong and they'll wonder why they just sat through your whole speech. Make it punchy, make it memorable.

## MAKE AN IMPACT!

# Visual Aids

Our brains were built for visual information:

90% of the information processed by the human brain is visual. Therefore, the human brain remembers only 10% of what you say alone so everything visual which is body language, expressions, gestures and movement as well as visual aids are very important to the effective delivery of a speech.

So, what are your visual aids in addition to your performance?

They could be anything from props, costumes, flip charts, pictures, posters as well as slide decks such as Google slides or PowerPoint.

The most important thing to remember is that these are NOT your crutch - if it all went wrong and they weren't there, you could still deliver the speech. The idea is that the Visual Aids support you but they don't do your job for you. It is essential to remember your slides are there for your audience NOT for you. Does each slide help your audience better understand what you are saying? If not, scrap them.

How many times have you been sat in assemblies or talks only to see the speaker read to you a whole load of text from their PowerPoint? Worse still, they turn to read it, delivering to the screen and not even their audience? Even worse still, they do this from behind a lectern! I know I sit there reading ahead of them and you probably do too. If your text is on the slide then you may as well go home and we'll read the notes instead.

You know how it feels for an audience member to have to sit through these types of talks, so don't do the same. Some speeches you encounter will serve as warnings rather than examples; watch as many as you can and learn from them. The best examples can be found on TED TALKS and TOASTMASTERS on YouTube.

Go back to the TED TALKS & TOASTMASTERS with this in mind; How do they use their visual aids? How do they interact with them? If the speaker gets this wrong, it may look as though there is some unrelated slideshow going on in the background. This is very important otherwise it will feel that some unrelated slideshow is going on in the background.

How many slides then? I would suggest a new slide for each new thought or idea. With regards to a maximum number of slides, you use as many as you need but no more. Each slide serves its purpose.

## Slide Deck Rules

- Use only one image per slide.
  The audience know where to look and it is not overly cluttered – a good rule is, it should not take longer than 3 seconds to take in the information on the slide.

- As little text as possible – Use key words and images to help illustrate your point.

- If a graph is used zoom in, show us where to look rather than the whole image.
- Use appropriate fonts and don't use more than 2 font types.

- Nice clear slides no fancy designs, templates and animations or transitions. Less is more.

- Size fonts appropriately - Don't use a font that is TOO BIG or ᴛᴏᴏ ꜱᴍᴀʟʟ. Your presentation is for people with normal eyesight…think about the space you will present in and design for the person at the back of the room. Try sitting there and test it out, if they cannot read it clearly they will switch off or give all their attention to trying to read the text that they will not be listening to you.

- Interact with your visual aids, they are not a fancy back drop for you – they should be relevant and referred to.

- Leave a pause for a few seconds when changing a slide. Your audience can focus on you OR your slide so let them take in the information before you start speaking (Great opportunity to glance at notecards).

  - The idea to remember is that the audience have come to see and listen to YOU. Your slides help illustrate your point.

- Keep your slides minimal not too cluttered and with as little text as possible.

- Stick to one image per slide. Two or more might leave the audience unsure where they should be focusing.

- Think about the position of your images, divide the screen into a grid 3x3 – where the lines intersect is the prime position.

- Think about varying font size to direct the audience's attention to key words or data.

- Value empty space  - don't cram your slide full of images or text

- Use image bleed – this means make your image fill the slide, it's more impactful.

- Create images that appeal to emotions and serve as reminders for your speech. Use high quality images!

   See the difference in impact of these two examples:

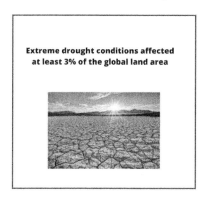

# YOUR EXAM

Grades 1-3

## Introductions

Imagine you have just stepped into the exam room. How do you feel? As well as feeling very excited, ok, nervous, you need to take a deep, slow calming breath and ensure that your entrance is professional and measured.

Walk in head up, back straight (refer back to the Body Language section we covered earlier). Make eye contact and smile at the examiner whist saying a warm "Good morning/ afternoon".

### Introduce your speech

It is expected that you will have a nice clear shape to your speech, a structure as we explored earlier. Your presentation should begin with a clear and separate introduction which may go something like this:

Good morning / afternoon. My name is …… and my first speech is called "why you must visit Rome"

Grade 1

**Time allowance – 15 minutes**

Grade one asks you to create a speech on a visit, trip or experience… this could be your voyage around the world, your day trip to Alton Towers or your cousin's wedding.

Visual aids may be used to help the speech but will not be marked – NO POWERPOINT or similar.

## What are they looking for?

The examiners want to see you deliver
confidently a speech about a favourite
event, holiday or trip and at this level you
may have a tendency to hide behind or
overly rely on your PowerPoint to do the
work for you – read the 'presentations'
section and you will understand why
LAMDA prefer you to employ these
methods further down the line when you
have greater skills.

Remember you don't have to use Visual
Aids but they may assist you so what
Visual Aids could you use?

- Costume
- Props
- Pictures
- Flip chart

# Interpretation

## L01 Prepare and deliver a speech demonstrating an understanding of the subject matter

|  | PASS | MERIT | DIST |
|---|---|---|---|
| 1.1 Give a prepared speech about an experience, event or visit using appropriate vocabulary & a clear structure | **Some of the time** | **Most of the time** | **All of the time** |
| 1.2 Demonstrate knowledge of the chosen subject | **Some of the time** | **Most of the time** | **All of the time** |

# Technique

## L02 Use the skills required for Speaking in Public

|  | PASS | MERIT | DIST |
|---|---|---|---|
| 2.1 Speak with audibility appropriate to the performance space | Some of the time | Most of the time | All of the time |
| 2.2 Speak with clarity of diction | Some of the time | Most of the time | All of the time |
| 2.3 Use appropriate facial expression to support the content of the speech | Some of the time | Most of the time | All of the time |
| 2.4 Communicate with spontaneity | Some of the time | Most of the time | All of the time |

# Knowledge

## L03 Know and understand the techniques required for Speaking in Public

|  | PASS | MERIT | DIST |
|---|---|---|---|
| 3.1 Give an explanation of how the speech was prepared | **Some of the time** | **Most of the time** | **All of the time** |
| 3.2 Maintain Concentration in the conversation | **Some of the time** | **Most of the time** | **All of the time** |
| 3.3 Engage and respond appropriately to questions in the conversation. | **Some of the time** | **Most of the time** | **All of the time** |

## How you can prepare

Practice talking to your family, friends
even pets about your visit or trip. Imagine
they had never been and you are a travel
agent or tour rep trying to sell the idea to
them. How do you travel there? What does
that place offer? What did you enjoy? The
food? Culture? Activities? Music?
Customs? There's so much to tell us when
you think about it.

Start by putting the trip into context, why
did you go? When was it? How did you
feel about it? Who else went with you?
How did you travel there?

Then move on to tell us all about the place
and events themselves. Be descriptive,
paint a picture in our minds so we feel we
were there too. Is there room for a little
comedy anecdote? One of my students
talked about his trip to India to see family

and how his mother and sister were obsessed with shopping, going from one crowded market to another searching for bargains whilst he and his father spent most their holiday waiting for them!

Finally, conclude with how you feel about the visit. Would you go again? Would you recommend the place for others to visit and why?

As you can see there is a clear structure to that speech.

Grade 2

**Grade 2** asks you to create a speech based on an object. This I think, is the most exciting topic option; it really could be anything. It may be a bookmark that your great Gran has handmade for you, it could be a piece of equipment used for a sport or a harness for climbing. One student brought in a piece of Lego and delivered a speech on the history of Lego including some very interesting facts about the largest construction recorded or the amount of Lego pieces we would each have, if shared equally around the planet. I have even had a student create this speech based on his bed! No, he didn't bring his bed in, but some bedding and he started his speech pretending to be asleep!

See what I mean about interesting 'hooks'? This student began his speech lying under a blanket and acted as though he had awoken mid-exam. He told us all about why he chose his bed, why it was special to him. Then he went on to tell us about the history of the bed, how important sleep is for our wellbeing and discussed different styles of beds; from fun bed designs from castle and racing car beds to water beds to those who unfortunately are not lucky enough to have one. He lies back down and puts out a paper cup & sign that read "Hungry & Homeless"

**What is the examiner looking for?**

They want to see that you have done your homework – that you're not only able to talk about your object, but that you can demonstrate that you have researched on it too.

So, take your object and investigate far and wide so that you can share the information you have learned.

In this Grade your Visual Aids will be marked so make sure you use them; i.e. don't bring in the object and simply leave it on the side unreferred to throughout the speech.

# Interpretation

**L01 Prepare and deliver a speech demonstrating an understanding of the subject matter**

|  | PASS | MERIT | DIST |
|---|---|---|---|
| 1.1 Give a prepared speech about an object using appropriate vocabulary & a clear structure | **Some of the time** | **Most of the time** | **All of the time** |
| 1.2 Demonstrate knowledge of the chosen subject | **Some of the time** | **Most of the time** | **All of the time** |

# Technique

## L02 Use the skills required for Speaking in Public

|  | PASS | MERIT | DIST |
|---|---|---|---|
| 2.1 Speak with audibility appropriate to the performance space | Some of the time | Most of the time | All of the time |
| 2.2 Speak with clarity of diction | Some of the time | Most of the time | All of the time |
| 2.3 Use appropriate facial expression to support the content of the speech | Some of the time | Most of the time | All of the time |
| 2.4 Communicate with spontaneity | Some of the time | Most of the time | All of the time |
| 2.5 Demonstrate effective use of Visual Aid(s) | Some of the time | Most of the time | All of the time |

# Knowledge

**L03 Know and understand the techniques required for Speaking in Public**

|  | PASS | MERIT | DIST |
|---|---|---|---|
| 3.1 Give an explanation of how the speech was prepared | **Some of the time** | **Most of the time** | **All of the time** |
| 3.2 Maintain Concentration in the conversation | **Some of the time** | **Most of the time** | **All of the time** |
| 3.3 Engage and respond appropriately to questions in the conversation. | **Some of the time** | **Most of the time** | **All of the time** |

**Grade 3** requires a prepared speech delivered from memory on a hobby or personal interest. I have had students deliver speeches on Tennis, Football, Cricket, Karate & Bhangra dancing. You still can't use PowerPoint slides yet, but why would you need to? This level is crying out for you to bring in equipment and demonstrate some dance moves or the correct way to hold a cricket bat.

## What is the examiner looking for?

The examiner wants to see that you can structure a speech and deliver information, demonstrating research and subject knowledge. They want to see that you are developing your clarity and projection. The examiner needs to hear and understand what you are saying, so be sure to keep up with those vocal exercises!

# Knowledge

## How did you create your speech?

This is your opportunity to demonstrate that you have a sound knowledge of how a speech is created from a choice of topic and researched through filtering of ideas and structuring into the speech they are watching today. You will need to explain the process you went from to create the finished pieces; this includes any ideas you dismissed and why.

## Conversation

Grades 1-5 require students to engage in a conversation with the examiner. In Grades 1-3 the students can offer their own topics.

Some topics my students have chosen previously for their own choice have included;

- Technology
- Hobbies
- Music
- Trading Card Games
- Sport
- Lego
- Holidays
- Transport
- Theatre
- Films and TV
- Advertising
- The Monarchy
- Reality TV
- Fashion
- Education
- Family
- Religious Holidays
- New Year's resolutions
- Food and drink

# Interpretation

**L01 Prepare and deliver a speech demonstrating an understanding of the subject matter**

|  | PASS | MERIT | DIST |
|---|---|---|---|
| 1.1 Give a prepared speech about an experience, event or visit using appropriate vocabulary & a clear structure | **Some of the time** | **Most of the time** | **All of the time** |
| 1.2 Demonstrate knowledge of the chosen subject | **Some of the time** | **Most of the time** | **All of the time** |

# __Technique__

**L02 Use the skills required for Speaking in Public**

|  | PASS | MERIT | DIST |
|---|---|---|---|
| 2.1 Speak with audibility appropriate to the performance space | **Some of the time** | **Most of the time** | **All of the time** |
| 2.2 Speak with clarity of diction | **Some of the time** | **Most of the time** | **All of the time** |
| 2.3 Use appropriate facial expression to support the content of the speech | **Some of the time** | **Most of the time** | **All of the time** |
| 2.4 Communicate with spontaneity | **Some of the time** | **Most of the time** | **All of the time** |

# Knowledge

## L03 Know and understand the techniques required for Speaking in Public

|  | PASS | MERIT | DIST |
|---|---|---|---|
| 3.1 Give an explanation of how the speech was prepared | **Some of the time** | **Most of the time** | **All of the time** |
| 3.2 Maintain Concentration in the conversation | **Some of the time** | **Most of the time** | **All of the time** |
| 3.3 Engage and respond appropriately to questions in the conversation. | **Some of the time** | **Most of the time** | **All of the time** |

# Level 2

Grades 4 & 5

## Introduce your speech

Good afternoon. My name is ...... and my first speech is entitled ....... The purpose of my speech is ....... My target audience is ...... The setting of this speech is ......

As you can see, there is much more detail in the introduction at level 2. Now examiners want to see that you have a clear purpose and target audience. I always suggest that students add in the context of the speech i.e. a speech in a hall for a whole school assembly would be quite different from the presentation of a pitch to a small group of school governors.

At this level, students are tasked with preparing and presenting TWO speeches.

Grade 4

The first prepared speech from memory is based on one of the following topics:

- **My favourite film**
- **Family Life**
- **The environment**
- **Someone I would like to meet (Past or present)**

For example, I have had students choose the Marvel films or Star Wars for the first option. Sibling rivalry or being an only child has been used for the second. The third option has developed exploration of global warming, pollution and the impact on wildlife caused by plastics in the ocean. The last option, I have seen a student create a piece on meeting Socrates and the questions he would ask him were he to meet him now in 2020. So, there are just a few ways that these titles have been interpreted, what other ideas do you have?

The second speech is on a topic of your own choice. Make it about something you are passionate about and a contrast to your second speech. For example: if your second speech is going to be a persuasive speech, perhaps think of making your first speech an informative one? What are you knowledgeable about? Is it a sport? Hobby? Place? Is there something that you feel really passionate about? Something you would really like people to consider. The freedom of choosing your own topic makes this an important decision to make.

This is your opportunity to discuss something you care about. If you don't care about it, the audience won't either.

A controversial question is always a good starting point to get those creative juices flowing. One student recently chose the question "Can we separate the Art from the Artist?" This speech started by a slideshow presentation of some famous faces, displayed one by one whilst the student told us of the celebrity's remarkable achievements and successes which he then morphed into telling us of the terrible atrocities of which they have been accused. His hook ended with posing the question "Should we cancel the creative work of these artists because of their personal behaviours?"

The body of his speech went on to explore how art forms, be they paintings, music or any other are a reflection of the artist, they are not stand-alone products. His call to action asked his audience to consider how poor a world would we be without the paintings of Picasso or the music of Michael Jackson?

Again, the first speech is based on a list of options:

- **Competitions**
- **Robots**
- **My favourite writer, artist or musician**
- **Keeping healthy**
- **Travel**

Students at this level have explored subjects such as whether competition is healthy, or by creating Artificial Intelligence actually creating our own doom? Driverless cars...are they safe? One favourite artist was a Japanese writer who suffered his whole life from depression and poured this into his work, posing the question does the best art come from suffering?

We've had the effect of exercise on the brain for the keeping healthy option, I have had students exploring the effects of exercise on the brain, especially with a focus on revising for exams. Finally, the topic of travel has seen students 'taking us' to Bali, India, Italy and explored how the best education happens outside of the classroom.

The second speech again, is based on your own choice. **Speeches must not exceed 4 minutes in length**.

## Knowledge:

**For both Grade 4 and 5 you will be asked about**

**Reasons**

- Why did you choose the topic?
- Is it something you have always had an interest in?
- Is it a personal passion for you?
- Have you covered it in school and want to explore it further?
- What aspects of that topic particularly inspire you?

139

**Research**

**Some questions to consider here are:**
- What sort of research did you do to gather your information for your speech?

At first you mind mapped everything you already knew but where did you go next and what did you find out?

To simply say the internet is an unhelpful answer.

- Did you go to specific sites?
- Why those sites? Were they more reliable, up to date or accurate?
- What did you find out?
- Did you use that information in your speech? If so, where and why? If not, why not? Was it interesting but took your speech off on a tangent?
- Where else did you research? Did you interview or discuss the topic with

people? Did you watch documentaries? Films? Did you read any articles?

There are a lot of sources for research so don't simply say "the internet"

## Conversation on unseen topics

At grades 4 & 5, the examiner provides the student with 3 unseen topic choices to initiate a conversation.

It really doesn't matter what your conversation topic is. If you practice the shape of a conversation, then you can apply that to anything thrown at you.

- Observation on topic
- Leading into 1st open question for the examiner
- Listen to their response
- Respond to their comments and move conversation forward to your next question.

- The examiner may have questions for you too.
- Finally summarise and draw to a close.

So, a conversation on pets could start;

I have always had pet dogs and think that they are more than just 'animals'. They are family. How do you feel about families having pets? Do you ever actually "own" a pet? How big a responsibility do you think owning a pet is?

# Conversation topics you could practice:

- Food and drink
- Holidays
- Languages
- School Uniform
- Animals
- Friends
- Happiness
- Social Media
- Education
- Technology
- Music
- Sport
- Hobbies
- Computer Games
- Mistakes
- Awards
- Opportunities
- Extra-curricular activities
- Peer pressure
- Swearing
- Voting

# Level 3

## Grades 6, 7 and 8

Grades 6 and above require an impromptu speech

The Impromptu Speech
Students are required to deliver an impromptu speech. Scary huh? Not really, because when you have progressed this far up the grades you are so familiar with writing speeches, you could probably do them in your sleep! You are so familiar with the structure of a speech and the techniques to employ that it really doesn't matter what topic you are given you will be able to create a speech. Firstly, you will never be given a topic that requires subject specific knowledge such as 1950's cars or the Vietnam War. Instead, you will be given open topics that any student could

take on any level. There will be three choices:

- A contemporary topic. For example, this could be "the environment" or "Social Media" this directs the content of your speech to a certain degree.
- An idiom or phrase. For example: A Man's best friend" or "Fashion tells people who we are"
- An abstract topic. For example: "Imagination", "blue", "time", "the future" "Fear"

You are given 15 minutes to prepare, during which I would recommend exploring all areas and you will find a focus that suits you. Yes, the content is important but it's not the main focus, they don't expect it to have the detail or finesse of your prepared speeches.

Your speech should;
- Be 2-3mins max.
- Show intention and purpose
- Clearly target a specific audience
- Have a clear structure
- Have impact
- Stay within the set time limit

This will come with practice. Set your timer for 3 mins several times not only when working on speeches and you'll soon just get a feel for how long 3 minutes is.

You will be given 15 minutes in the room with the examiner to work on your impromptu speech, bring a pen, paper and blank notecards.  Here's how to spend that time:

- Quickly make a decision on the topic, either because one appeals to you or by a process of eliminating those you dislike. I had one student overjoyed because one of her options was living without animals and she was currently studying animal extinction in Geography! So, if there is something you already know a lot about that is awesome. If not, most of the topics offered allow for a wide range of interpretation.

- Mind map initial thoughts- again do not spend more than a couple of minutes on this. A focus should become clear.

- Choose your purpose and target audience. You now have something to base your vocabulary, terminology and presentation on.

- Draw your boxes – Hook, Body and "Call to Action" and complete with bullet points

- Practice your ending, then your beginning and finally your body.

- 3 mins left – run through, how will you move in the space available?

I always suggest that students ask to present their Impromptu first, it gets it out of the way whilst still fresh and saves you trying to remember it whilst presenting your prepared speeches. Students have almost always scored full marks for this section. It really isn't as scary as you might think.

# Impromptu titles to practice

- Fear
- Hope
- Should footballers take a pay cut?
- Our shrinking world
- Animals – is it cruel to train them to obey you?
- Space
- Why toilet roll should be banned
- Crime & Punishment
- Food & drink
- Performance enhancing drugs in sport
- Is a sense of humour important?
- Travel is the best educator
- Colour affects our mood
- Poor health begins in the mind
- Poverty
- Separating the art from the artist
- Our brains are foolish
- Blue

- Technology is manufacturing our own doom
- Communication
- If I ruled the world
- Imagination
- Uniform
- Money makes the world go round
- Aliens exist
- Status
- The best invention
- Is trying to take over the world such a bad thing?
- If I had a superpower
- Why we love the misfortune of others
- Social Media

Grade 6

For their first speech students are asked to create and deliver a speech on a contemporary issue.

So what issues are relevant today, here and now? My students have covered such issues as homelessness, poverty, education, the voting age, fake news and the UK's response to COVID-19. It really can be anything providing it is currently affecting people or places and is unresolved.

The second speech is on a subject of the student's own choice; this is often the trickiest as it is so open. Think about a topic that is of interest to you and will contrast well with your first speech. So, for example, if you have picked quite a solemn subject for your first speech, a persuasive or political piece; think about making the second piece more informative with a lighter tone. You want to demonstrate that you can deliver speeches of varying tones and topics. My students in the past have chosen to cover subjects like 'the way people behave in a crisis and why', 'Conspiracy theories', 'The benefits of taking up Martial Arts'. The world is your oyster and sometimes that makes it difficult to choose; but this free choice category is really here to allow you to talk on something you feel passionately about. Think about the theme of Ted Talks 'ideas that matter'. What matters to you?

The third piece is the impromptu speech. (Refer back to earlier in this section)

## Knowledge

### Q1: The techniques involved in speech production and projection

As we know we speak on an out breath or exhalation – so the first thing we need to speak is air.

The **diaphragm**, a domed band of muscle located just beneath the ribcage, contracts, flattening it out. It is continuously moving up and down gently as we breath but to take in a deeper breath the diaphragm flattens and the **abdominal** muscles relax, moving outwards. At the same time the **intercostal** muscles, between the ribs, lift the ribcage up and outwards. This is why, if you are using diaphragmatic breathing correctly, your stomach will move outwards. Try it. Place your hand gently on your stomach and slowly breathe in as deeply as you can, totally filling your lungs. Your hand should be pushed outwards by your abdominal muscles. By all these muscles working in this way they cause a lower pressure in the **Thoracic cavity** creating a vacuum which sucks air into the **lungs**.

Now, when you exhale ready for your speech, the reverse happens, the intercostal muscles return the ribcage to their original position, the abdominal muscles contract and the Diaphragm relaxes returning to its dome shape. This pushes the air out of the lungs and up the **Trachea** or windpipe. Here it passes the **Larynx** / voice box /

vocal cords and if we wish to speak, we vibrate the cords / vocal folds. Now, it is easiest to picture the vocal cords as guitar strings. The more they stretch the thinner they are, the higher the pitch. The more relaxed, the thicker, the lower the sound that is produced. This vibration / sound moves upwards into the Pharynx and oral and nasal cavities where it **resonates**. Resonance is the quality or richness given to the initial sound by it being amplified bouncing around the oral 'cave'. Now without opening the door to the cave that sound would stay there but the wider we can open our mouths the easier it is for the sound to travel out to its audience. This unobstructed sound released produces vowels - which are great but not that useful on their own. So, we need to create consonants for the magic to really happen. This is done by employing the articulators:

- The lips
- The teeth
- The tip of the tongue
- The hard palate
- The soft palate
- The teeth ridge (behind the front top teeth)

Some of these cannot move so they are passive articulators, the others are active articulators moving into different positions to create different consonants.

You need **articulation** as well as **projection**. (Refer back to voice section)

# Resonance

Resonance is the amplification of sound through vibration in the hollow spaces of the nasal and oral cavities. The quality of resonance changes depending on how strong or weak the breath force is and how the speaker shapes and tenses the resonators. If breath force is strong, the sound will bounce off the hard palette and out through the lips - forward resonance. If breath force is weak it will only reach the soft palate and not travel far.

**The Pharynx:** This can change shape and size which affects the quality of sound. It increases during a yawn (so these are great!) and decreases when the neck is tense.

**Good Resonance:** depends on balancing between the Pharynx, mouth and nose. Head and chest resonance are secondary resonators and nothing to worry about. However, even though you now know this theory, try not to think about it when you speak!

**Q2: The techniques involved in organising materials for speeches including those presented**

This question is asking to see if you are confident in how you construct a speech from selecting a topic, to choosing your purpose and identifying your target audience. You will then need to describe the process you went through to create your speeches –refer to specific examples. How you mind mapped initial ideas such as … and then selected an area to research further. Where can you find sources for research? Now with a huge pot of ideas, how do you know which ones to use and which, as interesting as they are, to discard?

How do you then prioritise your ideas and filter further ensuring that you stay true to your purpose and audience? One suggestion is to pop each idea on a post-it note and place them on the desk, creating a through-line for your speech. This way you can see if your speech jumps around from one idea to the next or if the thoughts flow logically forward illustrating your point with greater clarity.

You have an order of ideas now you need to structure them into a speech. This is when you refer to your hook, body and call to action. What is the purpose of each? Give examples of strategies that you used to 'hook us in', how your ideas grew point to point with impact until BAM you hit them with your call to action!

**Q3: The techniques involved in matching topic, presentation and vocabulary to audience**

You need to break this one down, as you would any question with multiple parts. So, what do you 'do' to match topic to audience? Do you consider their background or current views / opinions? Their prior knowledge or understanding of the topic? Their level of understanding? What topic would be suitable for that audience. What do you think they either need or want to know? For example, a reception class are going to be taught about the importance of taking care of their teeth, not eating too many sugary foods, brushing regularly etc.

How do you think your presentation would differ if delivered to a reception class as opposed to a year 6 or a year11 class? Do you think they would be as interested in statistics, facts and figures? How long is their concentration span and how do you meet this? Think pace, visuals, vocal delivery, content.

What sort of vocabulary would you use with this audience as opposed to an older audience? If you pitch too low an audience will switch off, too high and they will get confused and yes you guessed it, switch off. So, it is really, REALLY important to know your audience and how you will meet their needs.

Grade 7

Grade 7 is not a million miles away from.
Grade 6. The requirements do increase
slightly - more on content and how you are
assessed rather than on being given a more
challenging task.

Your first speech will be based on a Moral
or Ethical issue – what does this mean?
Well, have you heard the phrase, "Just
because you can doesn't mean that you
should"? That might help keep you on track
whilst researching ideas for your topic.
Something may not be illegal but SHOULD
you do it? This is between you and your
conscience...topics could include 'should
we eat meat?', 'Should we give children the
MMR vaccine?', Is animal testing
acceptable?' Some of my students have
created speeches on "Should we give
money to the homeless?" "Should we buy
cheap?" or "Should grammar schools still
exist"?

In short, the best way to approach your ethical or moral issue is to pose a question. The purpose after all is to make your audience think.

Your second speech again is on a subject of your own choice. Use this opportunity to express your interest and in-depth subject knowledge be it about Ballet, stamp collecting or Rugby? I'm sure you can think of many more topics. One. One of my students has his own YouTube channel and gave a speech on making a career out of YouTube, how it all works. Fascinating.

Then your Impromptu speech – there is a whole section dedicated to this earlier in the book, so I won't go in depth here, but I do recommend you deliver that speech first. Immediately after your fifteen minutes with the examiner ask to deliver that speech so the ideas and drive are fresh and you don't have to keep them on hold whilst you deliver your other speeches. LAMDA examiners are happy for you to deliver in any order but just make it clear.

**Knowledge**:

**Q1: What is the value of the pause, emphasis and clarity of speech?**

Break this response up into sections so you ensure you cover each part asked. There are 3, Pause, Emphasis and Clarity of Speech.

**Pause**

What is it? What effect does using it create? What is the effect of no or too few pauses? What is the effect of too many pauses?

How do we know when and where to use pauses in our speech?

Give an example of a pause used in one of your speeches and explain your reason for using it.

Refer back to the vocal section to look at the power of the pause.

**Emphasis**, answer the same questions… what is it? Too little and too much can affect the speech in a detrimental way. How do we know where and when to use it? What techniques can we use to emphasise something? To make something stand out, elongate, pause before, after or both, add greater power or stress. Is there an example you can give from one of your speeches? Refer back to this section earlier in the book.

**Clarity of speech** – articulation, what is it? Why is it important and how is it achieved? Refer back to Grade 6 work on speech production.

Also include the importance of looking after your voice and using it properly when you are a public speaker.

**Q2: Tell me about the techniques required for effective audience communication (Including eye contact, use of note cards and body language)**

'**Techniques required**' means what do you have to do.

So, what do you have to do to ensure you effectively communicate with your audience?
Earlier in the book we talked about how to engage with your audience, the importance of it and how it can be achieved. This information will aid you with this response.

**Q3: Tell me about the research undertaken to prepare the chosen speeches.**

It is handy to keep a journal throughout your progress when creating a speech. Why are they asking this? Because they want to know that you wrote your speech based on research done and that you used a wide range of resources. Even if it was solely the internet try and talk about the different sites you used and why? Were some more official and likely to have up to date information? How did you filter this information and select which was most relevant for your topic? How did you order your ideas and prioritise? Explain this.

**Your first speech this time is on the process of preparation for your impromptu speech**

What was the system you followed during your 15 minutes with the examiner?

Refer back to the section on Impromptu speech preparation. Simply explain how you worked. What decisions you made, the purpose and audience, for example, how you structured your piece & used your time.

You have 15 minutes so plan how you will divide your time between the tasks. A typical allocation of time might look like;

Up to 1 minute to decide on a topic

2 minutes mind mapping initial ideas then identify the area you would like to focus on

2 minutes - choose purpose and audience – make decisions regarding the content of your speech and delivery to meet both of these.

7 minutes structure speech and ensure it has a clear purpose, clearly targets audience and has an impact. Divide your time, i.e. how long for the hook? Body? Call to Action?

2-3 minutes – run through it

# Types of speech

**There are five types of speech that
we will look at:**

- Persuasive
- Informative
- Political
- Humorous
- A vote of Thanks

## Persuasive

A biased speech aiming to persuade the
audience of your viewpoint. Do not start by
immediately promoting your viewpoint as
your audience will put mental barriers up,
they have their own opinions on the
subject, possibly deep rooted. You should
first identify where they are coming from,
point out the problem you have decided to
cover and then offer a possible solution.
Finally, the benefit of them listening to you
– you can use facts, data and statistics to
prove your points. If you can't back
yourself up with evidence it's unlikely your

audience will want to follow your way of thinking.

## Informative

Un biased – This is a speech that educates or informs about a given topic. You do not share views or opinions on it but rather demonstrate the facts as they stand.

Here are 2 examples of Informative speeches

Excerpt from Marie Curie's speech on the discovery of radium:

I could tell you many things about radium and radioactivity and it would take a long time. But as we can not do that, I shall only give you a short account of my early work about radium. Radium is no more a baby, it is more than twenty years old, but the conditions of the discovery were somewhat peculiar, and so it is always of interest to remember them and to explain them. We must go back to the year 1897. Professor

Curie and I worked at that time in the laboratory of the school of Physics and Chemistry where Professor Curie held his lectures. I was engaged in some work on uranium rays which had been discovered two years before by Professor Becquerel. ***I spent some time in studying the way of making good measurements of the uranium rays, and then I wanted to know if there were other elements, giving out rays of the same kind. So, I took up a work about all known elements, and their compounds and found that uranium compounds are active and also all thorium compounds, but other elements were not found active, nor were their compounds. As for the uranium and thorium compounds, I found that they were active in proportion to their uranium or thorium content.

President George W. Bush's address to the nation as the US attacked Iraq begins as an informative speech:
My fellow citizens, at this hour American and coalition forces are in the early stages

of military operations to disarm Iraq, to free its people and to defend the world from grave danger.

On my orders, coalition forces have begun striking selected targets of military importance to undermine Saddam Hussein's ability to wage war. These are opening stages of what will be a broad and concerted campaign.

More than 35 countries are giving crucial support, from the use of naval and air bases, to help with intelligence and logistics, to the deployment of combat units. Every nation in this coalition has chosen to bear the duty and share the honour of serving in our common defence.

## Political

For a political speech, whilst it remains persuasive you must remember that you are not speaking about solely your own views but rather representing the views of your party. Therefore, use 'we' rather than us.

Political speeches concern decisions about possible courses of action which are contentious and contested and about which people might reasonably disagree.

All of this means that your speech won't be about politics. It will be an instance of politics. You will be trying to win people's support for a proposition concerning something a community, a party, a council, a government, a country might do. It doesn't have to be a big thing though.

Your speech will be about something you think should or shouldn't happen, something that we might support or oppose

In drafting your speech, you should think about:
- what arguments might be significant for other people (not only the ones most persuasive for you)
- what people need to know about your proposition so that they can understand

and get on board with what you are
talking about
- the examples, data, quotations and other
kinds of evidence which will help make
your case
- the logical arguments – such as those
about principle – which can demonstrate
to people why your proposal is good and
right as well as likely to work
- the arguments people might make
against your proposal (so that you can
refute them in advance)

- how to make an audience pay attention
to you and to what you are saying
- how to engage people emotionally so
that they are motivated by your
arguments
- how to say things in a way that is
memorable, powerful and interesting

## Humorous

Best Man speeches are the most common
example of these – yes, be humorous, but
also be mindful. Self-deprecation or jokes

at someone's expense can be effective forms of humour in a Best Man's speech for example, but it's advisable not to target a wedding guest or you could be in danger of offending someone. However, as the best man, then you probably know the groom pretty well and how far you can go.

"Good afternoon everyone – for those of you that don't know me, my name's Scott and after all these years it's nice that Steve has finally admitted that I'm the best man!

I hope you've all had a lovely time so far and continue to have a fantastic time as the day and evening goes by – I'd also like to apologise in advance if I, in any way, ruin that in the next five minutes.

I know from personal experience that it's a difficult task choosing a best man, I'm still not sure about my choice four years on eh Steve?! But with Steve, like most things in life, it became more difficult as time went on – his first choice was his funniest friend but unfortunately, he said no, so then he thought he'd choose his cleverest friend but again, unfortunately the offer was declined. At the third attempt he turned to his most handsome friend but sadly it was a no yet again and at this point as you can imagine Steve was getting pretty desperate – that's when my phone rang! And, to be honest, hearing Steve's quivering little voice on the phone I decided I couldn't possibly turn him down for a fourth time!"

## Vote of thanks

This follows the key speaker, so it is a brief thank you to them. You will bring up highlights from their speech and comment on what you have learnt and how that will help you going forward. Say something kind but honest.
Finally, ask others to join you in thanking them and either wishing them all the best or stating how you are looking forward to their next talk.

For example;

Thank you, Gladys, for that informative talk about growing roses. I have certainly learnt about the importance of soil types and will ensure that I use compost in future. I am sure we have all benefitted from your expert tips tonight.

Please join me in thanking Gladys and we wish you all the best for your trip to Kenya next month and we look forward to your talk on Rhododendrons in December.

# How we work & examples of students' speeches

It's always best to learn from looking at successful examples so to finish off I wanted you to see some of the speeches our fantastic students have delivered to date; They are by no means all of them but a sample to show the type of range and how we work. I of course need to add that this is just the way that I teach, all LAMDA teachers teach differently. There is no right way of teaching but we have fun and achieve results both in skill developed as well as LAMDA results.

I have been extremely lucky to have worked with some amazing students. Amazing because they have a really positive approach to any task set and always endeavour to produce work to the best of their ability. They work between lessons and this really is key in achieving the higher marks. It is really obvious who are the few students who do not practice their vocal exercises and work on their speeches between lessons. So, if you are going to start your LAMDA journey make the decision to "go big or go home" as they say. You may not be the loudest, most confident orator, that's ok, that's my job but the attitude you apply is your job!

**How we work**

We discuss the demands of the syllabus at that particular level, the Learning Objectives and the Mark scheme.

Then we find a suitable topic, one that ignites a passion. As we explored the topic MUST interest you or you will find the process excruciating as we work on it for a while. It is supposed to be fun as well as work as Stephen King points out in The Shining "all work and no play makes Jack a dull boy"
Although there is a lot of discussion initially, I like to get students up on their feet and trying out ideas as soon as possible so that standing to deliver a speech seems less daunting, especially for the quieter more reserved student. We walk around the room during vocal warm ups and when exploring using gesture, body language and

use of space from day one. We try out ideas and my question are always 'How did that feel?' You tend to know if something is effective if it just 'feels' right.

The room is a safe zone, what I mean by that is that there is no right or wrong, we are playing around with ideas together with no one else watching, we are both trying things and there is no judgement. So yes, I sometimes model ideas or suggestions they have made so that the student can see how it would look from an audience member's viewpoint. We play word games such as the yes-no game, answer my questions without saying yes or no, word association / word tennis game and talk for 30 seconds or a minute on such and such. Fun activities that develop quick thinking skills and helps to reduce tension.

When we have discussed and chosen a topic, we mind map it together before I send them off to research further. When the student returns with a wealth more of ideas we start to discuss them and what the purpose of the speech could be, who would need or want to hear this?

Then we prioritise the ideas which are most important to include and why? It is always a team effort but I encourage the student to really take ownership of what is included and how the speech is shaped. Can you fit all the ideas in or do you need to cut any? If so which?
Before we start nailing things down, we look again at the purpose and actually start with the end, the call to action as this needs to be impactful remember. Then the Hook which has to grab our attention and finally the body.

Here are a couple more examples of student's speeches that have earned them Distinctions

**Modern Slavery**

A student comes on and plonks down a sports bag, pulls out a pair of trainers and attempts to sell them to the audience in a

'Del Boy' style. "I'm not asking twenty, I'm not even asking fifteen but a tenner ladies and gentlemen, who would like a pair of genuine Adidas trainers for only a tenner? Of course, you would." He then drops the role play and asks throughout his speech on Modern Slavery "At what cost would we bag a bargain?"

## Life cycle of a star

The student walked on, catching various audience members' eyes and finally resting on one. "you're a star" he states. He searches again, finds another "and so are you sir - in fact you are all stars! But don't think you are so special, even that guy in the BMW tailgating you earlier is a star.... I mean literally a star." He went on to tell us how a star is born is a mesmerising speech that kept us engaged throughout. Finally, after explaining the process of how we are made from the same atoms as a star he finishes with "so maybe that is something special after all?"

**Trombone lessons**

One student whose speech was about his trombone assumed the role of a professional musician who plays with the Philharmonic Orchestra.... well if you're going to be someone, be someone big. The audience he chose was a school governing body and his purpose was to persuade them to introduce trombone lessons for the students. His speech included an explanation of the various parts of the trombone with a demo too. Your speech really can be as dynamic as you wish.

**VR in Medical Training**

A year 10 student chose to address a medical panel to attempt to sell them his latest VR invention. He told them of all the benefits this could offer the medical training for the student doctors as well as a means for patients in quarantine to connect with loved ones when they are unable to visit. Although this was his own fictitious product, it was quite feasible because it was based on real life research.


## The Philippines

Student enters and starts a timer on the board behind him that increases one number every 4 seconds. He begins by asking the audience about their favourite memory of Primary school, "was it running into the hall putting your arms out like this (He does so) and spinning around? Was it racing around the playground as Spiderman? Or was it finally sitting on chairs for assembly rather than the cold hard floor because you were now in year 6?"
He then goes on to explain that he is from the Philippines and he had been over recently with his family to visit. His aunt is a teacher, so they went to see the school she worked in and to his surprise it was so different from the primary school he had experienced in the UK. A shortage of books

and pencils, no school uniform, tatty desks and chairs... he then moves on to tell us about the living conditions for these children's families often dumpster diving for the evening meal. He ends his speech by reminding us just how fortunate we are to have such a wonderful education system and decent living conditions. He then stops the clock behind him and turns back to the audience saying, "Oh and that number there? That's the number of Filipino children who have died during this speech"

THAT'S how impactful a great speech can be. Words are powerful, use them to make a difference.

Good luck on your LAMDA journey!

# NOTES

Printed in Great Britain
by Amazon

81746062R00108